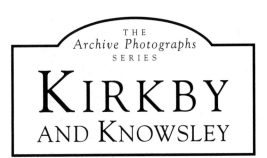

THE
Archive Photographs
SERIES

KIRKBY
AND KNOWSLEY

Kirkby Waterworks Tower and Boiler House, Tower Hill, 1953.

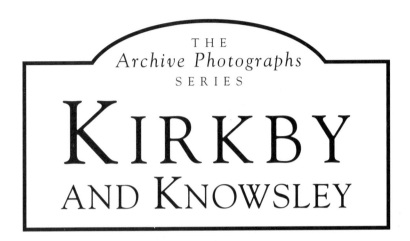

THE
Archive Photographs
SERIES

KIRKBY
AND KNOWSLEY

Compiled by
Michael K. Griffiths

CHALFORD

First published 1995
Copyright © Michael K. Griffiths, 1995

The Chalford Publishing Company
St Mary's Mill, Chalford,
Stroud, Gloucestershire, GL6 8NX

ISBN 0 7524 0349 4

Typesetting and origination by
The Chalford Publishing Company
Printed in Great Britain by
Redwood Books, Trowbridge

Kirkby Smithy, on the corner of Glovers Brow and Mill Lane, early 1900s.

Contents

Tenants of Knowsley Estate dancing on the lawn outside the Hall on the occasion of King George V's visit, July 1913.

Introduction

On 6 January 1066, 'the day King Edward was alive and dead', Kirkby and Knowsley were two townships in a block of some nineteen manors held by the thane, Uctred. They are mentioned in no surviving document earlier than the Domesday, much of their early history is far from detailed, though something may be inferred from other evidence.

Knowsley was settled before the end of the eighth century by the English from the north east and south west. Its name means 'Cynewulf's clearing in a wood'. It was including in Uctred's manors as part of a central block controlling the inland trade routes of what is now West Lancashire and Merseyside north of the Mersey. His other manors were placed along the coast, and at the river's mouth and the ferry crossings over it. This suggested Uctred held what would later be called a military fee, and thus may date back to the conquest of 'Between Ribble and Mersey' from the Norse by King Edward the Elder in the 920s. The subsequent history of Knowsley is largely that of the families of Lathom and their Stanley descendants. Since their earliest known estates match Uctred's so closely, many scholars have claimed them as his heirs. The 19th Earl of Derby still lives at Knowsley, which argues a continuity of ownership not paralled in England.

The Park is first mentioned in 1292, but no license exists for it, suggesting it is older. It has been extended repeatedly through the centuries, and it has swallowed the original site of Knowsley village, and that of Berry Hill, evidently once a fortification. A plan of 1776 shows scattered tenements, another of 1782, with later additions, shows some development of the modern site of the village, but is not until the first six inch Ordnance Survey map that the familiar layout is recognisable, for it is deliberate creation of the 13th Earl as a model village. The rest of the township has been altered most in the past thirty years, with the extension of the Cantril Farm housing estate over the Liverpool boundary. New houses are constantly being built, and even photographs from twenty years ago show barely recognisable scenes.

Kirkby has a much more complicated history. It was founded by Norse settlers from Ireland and Man at the turn of the ninth century. Sometime after the Norman Conquest, Uctred's direct heirs lost it, and in the middle of the twelfth century it was held by one Thurstan Banastre. On the failure of the male line it was partitioned between his heiresses and split into two moieties, later known from the families that held them as Kirkby Gerard and Kirkby Beetham. This division has left no trace today, and it is no longer possible to follow their boundaries, but for over a century after the reunification of the manor, the chapelwardens of St Chad's kept separate accounts. In 1565, Sir Richard Molyneux of Sefton purchased Kirkby

Gerard, while the grandson bought Kirkby Beetham in 1596. It was held by the Molyneux until it was sold by the last Earl of Sefton on 1947.

Improved drainage techniques from the sixteenth century onwards gradually increased the number of tenants and acres farmed. It was not until the mid-nineteenth century that there was any other class than yeoman, husbandman and labourer, when a few large houses were built in Kirkby by professionals who commuted to Liverpool. It was from that city that Kirkby underwent its greatest change since it was named by the Vikings.

In 1931, Liverpools population was 865,000 and climbing, while the major source of employment, the Docks, was in decline. Housing was poor and cramped. Liverpool had to diversify, expand and industrialise. Hence the great experiment of the outer estates. The history of that experiment as it pertains to Kirkby, and its mistakes, whose results we live with still, is told in the final chapter. It must be pointed out that, while usually taken as the archetype of the New Town, Kirkby, being the child of Liverpool alone, never received the full support of the state, as other, government sponsored projects did. Since 1974, Knowsley Council has had to earn its pay.

Some tribute must be paid to the people of Kirkby and their Borough that this artificial creation, crippled by the errors committed at its birth, did not collapse in the terrible years of recession and de-industrialisation, but yet became a community.

It is to the courage of that community that this book is dedicated.

Michael K. Griffiths

Kirkby railway station 1910.

One
Works and Days
Rural Kirkby

Harrowing, 1930s. While there are still a surprising number of farms in Kirkby, they are not what springs to mind when the name is mentioned. However, for the first thousand years of its existence, farming was all. The soil is excellent.

Kirkby Hall, Hall Lane, 1910. Never actually recorded as the seat of the lord of the manor, it was nevertheless the largest farm in Kirkby, occupied a central site next to the chapel, and the tenant — Nicholas Fazakerley — was of gentry status in 1650. It became temporary offices of Kirkby Urban District Council in 1958 and was demolished in the 1960s to make way for the present civic buildings.

Pear Tree Farm, c. 1920. This stood on the site of St Chad's Convent, one of the oldest farms in Kirkby. It was the birthplace of two very different clergymen. Peter Augustus Barnes was born there in 1786, and eventually took Holy Orders in the Catholic Church. Among his numerous achievements, he became Domestic Prelate to the Pope in 1825, and Bishop of the Western District in 1829. A skilled debator, he did much to assuage the hostility to the faith during the period leading up to Catholic Emancipation. The other resident was Robert Atherton, or 'Rob o' Bobs, the Ploughboy Poet' (see p. 87).

Cart and horses, 1920s. The system was to take the crop — in this case potatoes — to the agricultural market in Cazenau Street, Liverpool...

...and to return with manure.

12

Pigeon House, c. 1910. This is situated in the corner of Ingoe Lane and Whitefield Drive. It was built about 1703 at the same time as Whitefield House. It was a dovecot and, at least in the early years of this century, had a pigsty beneath it, to give the pigeons a bit of company. The photograph shows the original crenellation.

Whitefield House, 1960, was built in 1703 with some additions in 1770. By this century it had been divided into two dwellings. The north portion (right) ran the surrounding farm, and was known as Pigeon House Farm, after the dovecot.

Nanny Goat Hall, c. 1920. This stood on Kirkby Moss, east of the industrial estate, and was built of brick, with four rooms, the walls between them being made of corrugated iron lined with a mix of horsehair and plaster. It was the home of Annie Harrison as a girl, who recalled the headmaster of Knowsley School referring to her and her sisters as 'the Magi' because of the distance they had to travel.

Mill Lane, looking west from the bridge to Mill Farm, late 1950s. This was redeveloped in 1968 and is now a playground. Mill Farm is not to be confused with Mill Dam, although both were at times in the hands of the tenants of Kirkby Hall.

Charabanc, 1920s. For a small subscription the locals had an annual outing, usually to Southport.

Ploughing, Radshaw Nook Farm, 1920s. The site is near Shrogs Farm, by Junction 2 of the M56, and is now in Kirkby, but before the boundary was changed from the brook to the East Lancs in 1958, it was in Knowsley. 'Shaw' means wood, and 'rad' comes either from the colour (red) or from 'the great street' called Raddegate mentioned in some early Ingthwaith (whence Ingoe Lane) estate deeds. 'Shrog' means brushwood.

Farm labourers, c. 1910. The woman second from the left and the one on the far right may only be posing as workers, while the rest are the genuine article. About this time the pay and conditions were wretched, highlighted by the strike of 1913, when their demands were for £1 a week and a twelve hour day. After a small riot outside the Carters Arms near the station, where several people were injured and twelve labourers arrested, the strike was settled with a rise to the demanded twenty shillings a week.

Preparing potatoes for market, Sandy Brow Farm, 1920s. On the far right is Charles 'Charlie' Owen, and on the far left is his son. Owen's brother ran Little Britain Farm, now under the Industrial Estate.

Red Brow Farm, Bank Lane, 1960. This was obliterated by County Road, and stood just north east of the junction with Mill Lane. It was also known as Boyes Farm.

New Cut Farm, New Cut Lane, late 1970s. As drainage techniques improved from the sixteenth century, so more and more of the mossland in the east of the township was taken into cultivation, hence 'new cut'.

Woods' Patent Potato Shovel, c. 1910.
This celebrated (at least locally) wooden
shovel was designed and marketed by
Edward Woods, the village blacksmith
and wheelwright. Here he demonstrates
its strength.

Jack Kirby with a horse harnessed for ploughing outside the stable of Kirkby Hall Farm, c. 1920.
His family is recorded locally back to the seventeenth century.

Mr and Mrs Henry Hesketh of Boundary Farm, 1940. This was one of twelve farms taken over by the Ministry of Defence prior to the building of the Royal Ordnance Factory. This is said to have broken the hearts of this old couple, who died shortly afterwards.

Shepherd o' th' Hills Farm, Shevingtons Lane, 1960. Before the nineteenth century this property was known simply as The Hill, a rare feature in a landscape where the mildest rise was known as a brow.

Thatched cottage near Pear Tree Farm, near Bewley Drive and Little Brook Lane, c. 1940. Thatch was not common in this area because of the nearness of local slate.

Victoria Cottage, Delph Lane, c. 1900. The man in the photograph was Mr Smith who worked as a wheelwright at the blacksmith's forge.

Sandy Brow Farm, Sandy Brow Lane, c. 1950. This is not to be confused with Sandy Lane Farm, which is still in existence.

Cottage in School Lane (now County Road), home of the Shacklady family, 1912-1916. I am indebted to Mrs Shacklady for this and a number of other photographs in this book.

The Shacklady family and friends, c. 1912. On the left is John Shacklady, Edith Frances is the lady in the dark dress and Rachel is seated.

Two

Lord Derby's Estate

Five views of Knowsley village, 1950s, showing the Post Office, Church and Grand Lodge, all built in the 1840s, the Village Hall, built in 1897, and the War Memorial, 1920.

Maypole Green, c. 1950. The War Memorial is of Portland Stone and sixteen feet high. It was raised in commemoration of the thirty young Knowsley men killed in the Great War, including surprisingly, 'A. Denny, French Army'.

Maypole Green, 1970. Whether this was ever used as the ancient site of a maypole is very doubtful. It does not appear to have been common land, but rather the site of the village smithy, which names the croft in the Derby Estate Map of 1783. The tenant was William Woods. Probably the 'tradition' was artificially revived in the nineteenth century.

Estate Houses, Knowsley Lane, 1977. The village is an artificial one, deliberately built by the Earls of Derby in the last century. The buildings are sometimes difficult to date, as they are built in much the same style, but not all at the same time.

The Derby Arms, Knowsley Lane, 1910, soon after it was opened. The first tenant was James Hornby. Inns with this or the Eagle and Child name abound in the district. The latter are named after the Stanley crest. Legend has it that a child of a defeated king of Ireland who was rescued by an eagle and taken to Lathom Park was found and adopted by a childless lord of Lathom and became the ancestor of the Earls.

KNOWSLEY Church nr Liverpool.

St Mary's Church, c. 1890. From time immemorial Knowsley was part of the Ancient Parish of Huyton. The earliest chapel, which was in existence by the twelfth century at least, stood on Riding Hill, west of the entrance to the present Safari Park, but this had vanished by the Reformation. A Presbyterian (later Unitarian) chapel was established by 1717, near the corner of School Lane and Nunthorpe Road (hence Unity Drive). When the lease expired it was consecrated as a chapel of ease in 1830. However, the 13th Earl had bigger things in mind.

St Mary's, from Knowsley Lane, c. 1900. The Earl's daughter, Lady Henrietta Stanley, married a clergyman, Revd Francis Hopwood. From 1841 to 1844, the present church was built for him, at a cost of £20,000, but remained in law part of Huyton Parish, Hopwood being the Perpetual Curate, not Vicar.

Vicarage Lodge, Tithebarn Road, 1977. The Earl also built an impressive parsonage, now known as Dumbrees House. The present vicarage was built for his successors, who had less exalted in-laws. Knowsley became a parish in 1870.

Interior of the church, c. 1910, showing the unusual absence of a central aisle. There were two architects involved in its construction. Edmund Sharpe built the nave and the west tower and E.G. Paley added the transepts in 1860. After the death of the 14th Earl in 1869, the Derby Chapel became the place for all subsequent Earls to be buried.

The Derby Chapel, 1870. The effigy is by Matthew Noble and was erected by public subscription. It bears the legend, 'This monument is erected by his Tenantry in memory of Edward Geoffrey, fourteenth Earl of Derby, K.G., as a mark of affection and respect'.

Knowsley C. of E. School, Knowsley village, 1977. The earliest known school in Knowsley was founded by the second wife of the 1st Earl, Margaret, Countess of Richmond, mother of King Henry VII. This particular building was built in 1845 by the 13th Earl, who is said to have spent £100,000 on churches and schools at a time when the most prosperous labourer was lucky to earn three shillings (15p) a week.

Knowsley Lane, looking south, 1960. Stockbridge Lane is on the right. It is named after a wooden bridge over the River Alt, referred to as a boundary in 1189. Two other roads are mentioned: Siwardsgate, after an eleventh century Lord of Knowsley, and Leonardsgate, leading to the chapel on Riding Hill.

The Avenue, Knowsley Park, c. 1900. This private road was once known as Higher Road, and was the main highway from Huyton to Ormskirk. In 1776 the 12th Earl enlarged the Park, taking it to its present boundary in the west. To do this he had to improve Lower Road, making it into Knowsley Lane, and re-locate some of his tenants. This was the origin of the modern Knowsley village.

Huyton Lodge, c. 1910. On the night of 9/10 November 1843, Thomas Kenyon, gamekeeper at the newly built Huyton Lodge, was awakened by the park watchers, who claimed to have heard shots. When he caught up with the poachers, he recognised one of them as a former colleague and shouted his name. One of the poachers fired and Kenyon fell, mortally wounded.

The Avenue, c. 1910. The ensuing outcry jogged a lot of consciences, and one of the poachers turned Queen's Evidence. Four of the poachers were transported, and one, John Roberts, who fired the fatal shot, was hanged at Kirkdale 20 January 1844.

St Helens Lodge, also known as Eccleston Lodge and Park Lodge, 1914-1919. This stood on the site of the present roundabout at the junction of the Prescot by-pass and St Helens Road. This area was included in the Park in 1797, when the 12th Earl bought Parkside, the house by the hill east of the Safari Park entrance. It was later sold to Liverpool Corporation for the siting of reservoirs.

St Helens Lodge, c. 1910. Note the sign 'Beware Of The Bulls'.

The Bridge Lodge, also known as Knowsley Gate Lodge and Bridge. It was built in 1850, after a design by William Brown, who also designed many of the other lodges and much of Knowsley village. The other lodges guard the entrances to the Park; this is the only one inside the park walls, which also date back to this time.

The Grand Lodge, also known as Liverpool Lodge, c. 1900. The largest and most impressive of the lodges stood at the junction of Knowsley Lane and Stockbridge Lane. It was demolished in 1972 to make way for the M57.

The Tower, overlooking White Man's Dam, c. 1900.

The Boat House on White Man's Dam, c. 1910. The lake is artificial, either designed or improved by 'Capability' Brown, around 1775. It was originally known as the Great Water.

The White Man, c. 1900. Details are hazy, but the story is that this statue was fished out of the lake sometime in the early nineteenth century, prompting the renaming of the Great Water as White Man's Dam.

The Mizzy, or Little Dam, c. 1910. This is the source of Prescot, Logwood and Chapel Brooks, which eventually, as Ditton Brook, discharges into the Mersey.

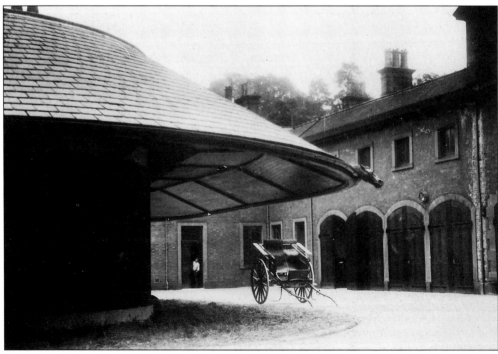

The Stables at Knowsley Hall, 1913, another of Burn's designs.

Three

Sefton's Folly
The County Cathedral

St Chad's Church and vicarage, c. 1910. There has been a place of worship here for over a thousand years. When the Norse settled here in the early tenth century, they called it 'Kirkja byr' — 'Churchtown'.

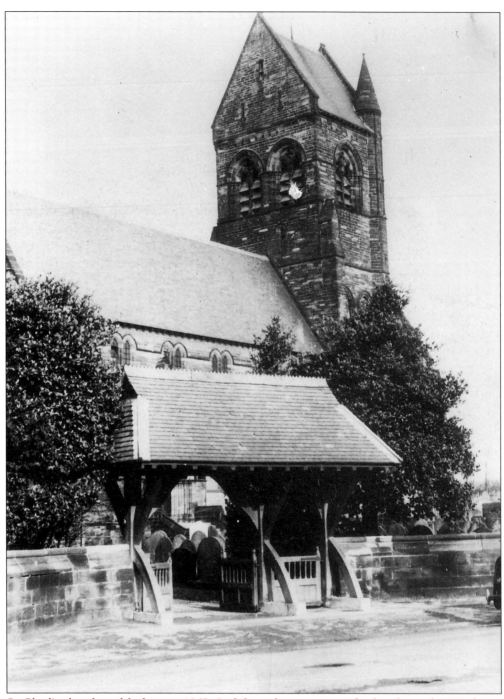

St Chad's church and lych-gate, 1963. It did not become a parish church until 1872, being anciently a chapel of ease in the large parish of Walton. It is dedicated to Ceadda (Chad) a seventh century saint who was successively Bishop of Northumbria and Mercia. His most endearing miracle was to absent-mindedly hang his cloak upon a sunbeam.

St Chad's Chapel, 1860. The ancient chapel having fallen into decay, the parson, Thomas Wilkinson, raised this building in 1766 at a cost of £1,043. It was enlarged by Revd Thomas Cope and T. Robinson, Lord Sefton's agent, at their own expense in 1812. The steps on the right which led to the south gallery were added in 1851. It had a capacity of 600 people when the population of Kirby and Simonswood was 1,910.

St Chad's, old and new, 1871. In 1868, the Earl of Sefton decided Kirkby was to become a great town, so it needed a church to match his aspirations. On 27 October, his tenants, representing 114 farms, voted to do a day's carting of sandstone for every four statute acres they leased.

The same churches from Old Hall Lane, 1871. The new chapel was consecrated in 1871, the last service in the old building was on 4 October, and it was demolished in 1872, the stones being used for the churchyard wall. A cross marks the site of the altar.

St Chad's Church and Kirkby village, c. 1900. The church dominated the landscape. It is here seen from what is now the junction of Hall Lane and County Road, a view that now requires a real leap of the historical imagination!

St Chad's Church from Kirkby Row, c. 1920. The incongruity of such a large building in a rural site led to it being called 'Sefton's Folly' and 'the County Cathedral'.

The font, c. 1900. This is the only memorial of the first chapel. The coil which forms the base is a serpent, between whose jaws the figure in the centre thrusts a spear. To the right of him is a figure with a sword. Just out of view are Adam and Eve. The remaining figures represent the different grades of holy orders.

The church interior, c. 1910. The architects were Paley and Austin and the furnishings were by Messrs Urquhart and Adamson of Bold Street, Liverpool. By tradition there was some dispute between the tenants of Kirkby and Simonswood as to the pillars. This was solved by having round pillars on one side and octagonal ones on the other. At any rate, at the Harvest Festival, Kirkby farmers decorated the round pillars, while those of Simonswood did the octagonal ones.

The old parsonage, 1930, later known as Beech Villa. This was built in 1733 by the curate, William Mount, who gave the communion plate. It was demolished in the 1960s.

The vicarage, 1977. This replaced the old parsonage in 1848.

The vicarage garden, 1913. On the right is Revd Crawley-Bouvey, who was vicar 1906-1913. On the left are Mrs James Mercer and Mrs Richard Mercer.

St Chad's organists, c. 1950, seen at Kirkby Cricket Club behind the village hall in Old Rough Lane. Left is William McCoy, headmaster of the village school, and right is Robert Bretherton, choirmaster.

St Chad's Lodge garden, 1930, and Richard Hesketh, who was born at the old village schoolhouse in 1869. His father, William, had been the schoolmaster, but quit to become a coal merchant. He was also parish clerk, in which office Richard succeeded him in 1906. Richard was also Local Government Tax Collector, Assistant Overseer of Sefton R.D.C. and Verger of St Chad's. He died in 1941 and Richard Hesketh Drive is named after him.

St Chad's Football Team, 1928, in which year they were runners-up in the Church of England League. On the left is Revd E.V. Fenn, vicar 1915-1928. On the far right is Walter French, one of the teams's founders.

St Chad's Church and Lodge, 1930s. The field was rented by the Temperance League to hold their field days.

St Chad's Choir, 1913. Front row, from left to right are: William Roberts (clerk), Joe Sumner, Edward Woods (blacksmith), James Holt (farmer), Anthony Bolton. Back row are: George and Albert Jones, Richard Hesketh (parish clerk), William McCoy (schoolmaster).

Mothers' Union tea party, vicarage lawn, c. 1939. Third from the left is Mrs Griffiths, the wife of the vicar who saw the transition of Kirkby from 1934 to the 1950s. The (blurred) lady on the right is their daughter, Joan.

The Drive, 1900. This was a private road constructed in the mid-nineteenth century by the Earl of Sefton between St Chad's and Croxteth Hall. The Molyneux were Catholics until 1769, when the 8th Viscount conformed. He was rewarded with the Irish Earldom of Sefton.

St Chad's Gardens under construction, 1965. The church has kept much of its character thanks to the 7th and last Earl of Sefton. When he sold Kirkby to Liverpool Corporation in 1947, he insisted that no building should take place within 200 yards of the church, so that, in the midst of the modern town, it retains some of its original rural setting.

St Chad's Gardens, 1969. The 4th Earl of Sefton's aims came to fruition: Kirkby did become a great town, and now 'the County Cathedral' is too small for the parish. Kirkby now contains some fourteen other places of worship.

Four
Vanished Scenes

Glover's Brow from Kirkby Row, c.1900. On the right is the station booking office, which was demolished in 1977. On the left is the coal depot, which later became part of the Railway Hotel.

The junction of Glover's Brow, North Park Road and Mill Lane, in the 1920s. The Carter's Arms is on the left, Woods' Smithy is in the centre. Behind the railing on the right was Dearbought Delph, an early nineteenth-century stone quarry, disused from the 1870s.

Glover's Brow, c.1900, showing the coal depot. Apart from such incidents as the 1913 farm labourers' strike, one policeman at this time was considered enough for Kirkby in those pre-'Z Cars' days.

Kirkby Post Office, Kirkby Row, c.1950. In 1873
the sub-postmaster was John Parkinson who was
succeeded by his wife, Ellen, until 1900, then
his daughter, Sarah to 1904.

North Park Road, c. 1915. At this time it was a cul-de-sac ending in a field just west of Number
40. On the south side were large residential houses dating back to the second half of the last
century and built by Liverpool businessmen.

Lytham House, North Park Road, c. 1905, built in the late 1860s by Christopher Wade, a Liverpool estate agent, as a retirement home. By 1890 he sub-let half of it to Dr Joseph Walker. Later occupiers were Robert Heaton in 1901 and Robert Burns in 1909. In 1913 it was owned by Dr Richard Ainsworth, whose sister, Katie, succeeded him, until 1987. It is named after Wade's birthplace.

School Lane, c.1900, looking north to Red Brow and Bank Lane. Alex Chorley, in his survey of 1696 calls it 'the great road from Prescot to Ormskirk'. It is now County Road.

School Lane, c. 1900, looking south. It was named after St Chad's School, and built in 1806.

Moor End (now Moor Lane), c. 1910. Just visible on the left is the New Inn. All this was demolished to make way for Valley Road in 1964.

The Cocoa Rooms, Kirkby Row, 1910. It stood almost opposite the present James Holt Avenue. It was built in 1735 as a café and meeting place, unusual in such a small village. It continued to serve refreshments, but by this century it was a general store, the only real shop in Kirkby. The first floor was hired out for meetings, hence its other name, Chapel House.

Glover's Brow, c.1900. Glover's Brow Farm stood approximately where Nos. 5-12 Mount Crescent now stand. The tenant in 1696 was Thomas Glover, aged 50. On the right is the building which later became a dairy.

Wilbraham Cottage, c.1900. Strictly speaking this was not actually in Kirkby, being just within Melling, the boundary being the garden fence. It stood on the west side of Prescot Road just after the last houses off Glover's Brow.

Wilbraham Cottage, c.1910. It is marked on the 1893 Ordnance Survey, but the earliest identifiable occupier in the directories is John McG. Lamb, in 1924.

Bank Lane, c.1910. This was known, in 1696, as Blackbank.

Kirkby Mill, c.1910. This was demolished in the late 1950s. The brook now known variously as Simonswood, Bank, Mill and Little Brook was dammed to make a watermill. In 1696 it was held by the Fazakerleys as part of the Kirkby Hall estate. There appears to have been a mill on the same site in 1323, but it was ordered to be thrown down as it was flooding neighbouring properties in Melling.

Mill Dam, 1930s. Kirkby was a popular resort for day-trippers from Liverpool. Mill Dam Lake was used for boating and swimming.

Mill Dam, 1930s, showing the Mill and the waterworks tower.

Mill Brook, undated. Being in a very marshy area, Kirkby was prone to thick mists and this photograph seems to show one of them.

The railway bridge over Mill Brook, looking north.

The St Helens Corporation Waterworks Tower, March 1964. This stood between the railway line and the running track north of Ruffwood School. In 1888 St Helens Corporation approached Lord Sefton with a view to constructing a pumping station for its increasing needs. He agreed, provided he approved of the design.

Waterworks tower, interior, c. 1918. The Borough Engineer, D.M.F. Gaskin, designed it as a medieval donjon. It was completed in late 1889. The tower itself, including the ornamental chimney, stood 110 feet high.

Waterworks Tower and surrounding farmland, c.1939. By the 1960s the tower was redundant, so it was demolished, but not before it gave its name to Kirkby's last estate, Tower Hill.

Opposite: Waterworks Tower, 1960. The building contractors were J. & T. Yearsley of St Helens. It contained over one million bricks and twenty cubic feet of stone. The walls were four feet thick.

Kirkby Railway Station, c. 1910. Built in the middle of the last century, it was extensively rebuilt in 1977.

Liverpool Corporation's Kirkby Estate Diesel Locomotive No. 4 hauling streamlined bogie cars over the estate railway, 10 November 1956. Good communications were vital in the decision to place the Royal Ordnance Factory in Kirkby, and hence in the choice of the site for the overspill estate.

Five

The 'Kings of Lancashire' at Home

Knowsley Hall, 1913, the seat of the Earls of Derby, and the Lathoms before them, for centuries.

The Garter Stall Plate of Thomas, 1st Baron Stanley (fl. 1406-59). In the first and second quarters of the shield are the arms of Lathom quartered with Stanley (the stags heads). By a truly amazing stroke of luck — the death of all his in-laws — Thomas' father, John, became heir to the Lathom holdings holdings in Lancashire, which his descendants have held since. They were also Kings and Lords of Man 1405-1735, hence the legs in the design.

Knowsley Hall, west front, c. 1950. The oldest part of the hall are the two round towers in the centre of the picture. They were built by the 1st Earl for King Henry VII's visits.

Edward, 12th Earl of Derby (b. 1752, s. 1776, d. 1834). This great sportsman founded the Derby and Oaks Races. Had he not extended the Park after succeeding the title, the modern Knowsley village would not be there.

Edward 13th, Earl of Derby
(b. 1775, s. 1834, d. 1851). He is
best remembered for his menagerie
which he employed Edward Lear to
record. It was in entertaining the
Earl's numerous young relations
that Lear invented the limerick.
The menagerie (when stuffed) and
his natural history collection
formed the basis of Liverpool
Museum.

Edward Geoffrey, 14th Earl of Derby
(b. 1799, s. 1851, d. 1869). He was
four times Prime Minister and
translated Homer, a hobby he shared
with Gladstone. He was actually
considered as a candidate for King of
Greece, but he didn't think it an
attractive option.

Edward Henry, 15th Earl of Derby, (b. 1826, s. 1869, d. 1893). He held a large number of posts in government. A liberal Tory, he joined the Liberals in 1880, but quit when Gladstone brought up Home Rule for Ireland.

Frederick Arthur, 16th Earl of Derby, he was born in 1841 and succeeded on the death of his brother. He was a distinguished Governor of Canada. He died in 1908.

Edward George Viliers, 17th Earl of Derby (b. 1865, s. 1908, d. 1948). He was Secretary for War in World War One and was best known for forming with Lord Kitchener 'the Pals' Battalions.

Edward John, 18th Earl of Derby (b. 1918, s. on the death of his grandfather 1948, d. 1994). He won the Military Cross at Anzio in 1944 and founded Knowsley Safari Park.

The Stucco Room, Knowsley Hall, 1949. The vase in the centre of the photograph is supposed to have been the very one Selima, the cat in Gray's *Ode on the Death of a Favourite Cat*, drowned in while trying to catch goldfish.

The Library, 1949. Among the treasures held is the prayer book of the 7th Earl and the drawings Edward Lear did of the 13th Earl's menagerie.

The State Dining Room, 1949. This was built by the 12th Earl in 1820-21. The great doors are big enough to grace a fair-sized church, which caused General Grosvernor to ask, 'Pray, are these great doors to be opened for every pat of butter that comes into the room?'

The chair the 7th Earl knelt on at his execution at Bolton 16 October 1651. The 1st Earl got the earldom for Richard III at Bosworth, while the 7th lost his head for his loyalty to Charles I, although, given his descent from Henry VII, he would have had a good chance of becoming King when Parliament despaired of the Stuarts.

King Edward VII and Queen Alexandria arrive at Knowsley Hall during their tour of Lancashire, 12 July 1905. The Hall has seen royal visits since the late fifteenth century.

King Edward VII and local dignitaries, 12 July 1905.

The 16th Earl's motor cars, 1902. From left to right: 12 h.p. Daimler, 5.5 h.p. Locomobile, 10 h.p. Wolseley, 10 h.p. Georges Richard.

Iceland ponies belonging to the Countess, 1902.

King Edward VII leaving the Hall, 14 July 1905.

The Knowsley tenants' Address of Welcome, recorded just prior to the arrival of King George V at Knowsley Hall, July 1913.

Knowsley Hall, July 1913. Here Edward Montague Cavendish, Lord Stanley, is talking to Mrs Wainwright, the housekeeper, who holds the bouquet she will give to Queen Mary.

Knowsley Hall, July 1913. Lord Derby and two unknown gentlemen.

Knowsley Hall, July 1913. King George V knights Mr Scott-Burnett, Chairman of Lancashire County Council, for services to the County Palatine.

Knowsley Hall, July 1913. The tenants of the Knowsley Estate file into the marquee for the celebration luncheon.

Knowsley Hall, July 1913, and the tenants are at lunch.

Six

Individuals and Institutions

Station Master's house, Kirkby, 1900, the first built of the Railway Cottages nearest Glover's Brow. Shown is Thomas R. Mort, Station Master from 1889 to 1910, with his family.

Little Brook Cottages, c.1925. Here Arthur Smith takes his dog through its tricks.

The New Inn, Moor Lane, c. 1910. Dating pubs is very difficult because the licences are in the tenants' names, but the name of the pub or where it is situated are not recorded. Baines' Directory of 1824 gives the tenant as Jane Molyneux. Another pub, now under the Industrial Estate, was the Little Briton, which gave its name to a hamlet in the south of Kirkby and also gives its name to the Britonwood part of the Estate.

Kirkby Football Team, c. 1920, who have obviously won something. The houses in the background are in North Park Road.

Mill Dam, 1952. There was a shortage of teachers after the War, so Liverpool opened an emergency college at the R.O.F. Hospital at Kirkby Park. By 1951 the immediate needs were supplied, so the Corporation offered the facilities to the Federation of Malaya. It closed in 1962. Here Mr Rimmer of Mill Farm poses with four students.

The Parish Hall, Old Rough Lane, 1937, at a Christmas Pantomime with members of Kirkby Girls' Club.

Members of Knowsley Cricket Club Team, 1908. The team was made up of a mixture of tenants of the estate and staff from the Hall.

Knowsley Hall, c.1920. Traditionally, Knowsley and Kirkby played a match at the Hall on a Whit Monday. The practice was abandoned during the War.

Members of Kirkby Cricket Team, c. 1930. The cricket pitch was taken over during the War and used for the construction of a hostel for the Royal Ordnance Factory workers. At the extreme left and right are the umpires, Edgar Woods and Joe Ledson. Fourth from the left on the top row is the Captain, Dick Gregson.

Glover's Brow, 1900. The invention of the motor car was followed by many strange experiments by amateur enthusiasts, knocked up by the local blacksmith. This car was designed by the man on horseback, Joseph Lamb of Chatham House, North Park Road. Either it has broken down, or he had not grasped the principles of the internal combustion engine!

St Chad's School, c. 1930. There was an ancient school in Kirkby, built on the land attached to the parsonage. The schoolmaster was endowed with £8 a year from rent on a house in Billinge (hence known as the Billinge Charity), left by one Nehemiah Crawley. This school burned down some time in the eighteenth century and children were taught in the vestry.

St Chad's School pupils, c. 1913. In 1806, Lord Sefton built this school at a cost of £448, 11 shillings, 1 penny and three farthings. The schoolmaster received £40 a year.

St Chad's School pupils, c. 1912. The school was enlarged in 1851. The old building was used as the boys' school and the addition for the girls.

St Chad's School pupils, 1917. In 1850, the average number of pupils was 60 boys and 110 infants.

St Chad's School pupils, 1917. Being an agricultural township, everybody pitched in at harvest time. The school log book often mentioned that an insufficient number of pupils had turned up and the school was closed until the crops were gathered.

Robert Atherton, "the Ploughboy Poet", c.1925. He was born at Peter Tree Farm in 1861. Entirely self-educated, he became Vicar of Bolnhurst, Bedfordshire in 1888, but he was too weird for his flock, who managed to get him dismissed on suspicion of being too familiar with his boy bellringers. He eventually returned to Kirkby and became a ploughman. He wrote a great deal of verse. He died in 1930.

Knowsley Hall, 1913. On the left is Lord Herbert Vane Tempest, second son of the Marquess of Londonderry. On the right is Captain the Hon. Algernon Francis Stanley, seventh son of the 16th Earl of Derby. He had already had a distinguished career in the Life Guards, serving in the Boer War. The next five years of his life were to be eventful ones, winning the D.S.O. in the following year.

1st City Battalion, King's Liverpool Regiment at Knowsley Hall, August 1914, at the start of the Great War. They will shortly land in France as part of the British Expeditionary Force and by November they will have suffered eight hundred casualties.

'Back to the Land', the 3rd City Battalion, at Knowsley Park, c. 1919. In theory there were fifty seven battalions of this regiment during World War One, but enormous casualties meant that the number in service at any one time was much less.

Presentation of the King's Police Medals at Knowsley Hall, 13 July 1951. The 18th Earl of Derby, acting as the Lord Lieutenant of Lancashire presents the medal to Mr A.W. Fothergill, Second Assistant Chief Constable of Liverpool.

Opposite: Knowsley Park, 21 July 1958. Here Lord Derby presents gold watches as long service awards to some of the house staff.

Presentation of the King's Police Medals at Knowsley Hall, 13 July 1951.

Knowsley Playing Fields, Knowsley Lane, 13 June 1958. Lord Roseberry, a lifelong friend of the 17th Earl, opens the cast iron gates built as a memorial to him, ten years after his death.

Seven

The Royal
Ordnance Factory

View of the factory from the observation post, looking east, October 1945. The coming of World War Two meant an enormous demand for bombs and shells. Because of the dangers of working with high explosives, a rural site with good communications was required and 743 acres were taken in Kirkby.

The main entrance to the Administration Building, October 1945. There were no plans drawn up before September 1939. Preliminary planning was done at Woolwich Arsenal. Sir Alex Gibson was the consultant, Holloway Brothers the contractors. It was completed in January 1941.

View from the observation post looking south west, October 1945. Lawrence Gale from Woolwich Arsenal was appointed Superintendent in July 1940, taking nine staff with him. The first shell came off the production line in September 1940. There were between 50 and 100 employees when it opened.

Wages Office, Administration Building, October 1945. The factory cost over £8,500,000. By the summer of 1941, 10,000 people were employed, rising to a peak of 20,000, most of whom were women. Many staff transferred from Woolwich after that was bombed. A Y.W.C.A. hostel was built next to Kirkby Station for 1,000 women.

Railway line, passenger platform, north west entrance, October 1945. There were three trains from Liverpool every shift. The factory also had an internal bus service.

Main gate from the south west, October 1945. With so many employees coming from Liverpool, the Corporation had to extend its bus and tram services to the factory, buying old buses from London to fill the gaps. Until 1943 they were marked 'Simonswood' to confuse saboteurs.

Part of the loading bay, October 1945. In 1940-41, the factory concentrated on anti-aircraft ordnance to counter the Blitz; in 1941-42, anti-tank ammunition and mines for North Africa; in 1942-43, H.E. bombs and mines for the bombing of Germany.

Machine Shop, October 1945. In 1943-44, it concentrated on supplies for D-Day and the French campaign.

Kitchens, canteen, October 1945. To reduce the risk of fire, three canteens were originally situated outside the factory, but this was inconvenient and reduced production. The problem was solved by cooking the food in outside kitchens and then transferring it to internal canteens.

Canteen, October 1945. No part of the factory was lost to enemy action, although some bombs dropped close by. However, accidents did occur.

Components sheds, October 1945. On the 22 February 1944 at 8.20am, a tray of fuses for anti-tank mines exploded, wrecking the building. One girl was killed, another died of injuries and a third was seriously injured.

Interior of Boiler House No. 1, October 1945. Factory Dept. Officer R.A.S. Bywater and three assistants removed and checked the remaining fuses. Twenty three were found to be critically defective and an especially sensitive one was carried by Bywater to a sandbagged safe. He was awarded the George Cross, while his assistant received the British Empire Medal.

Main Fire Station, October 1945. On the night of 15 September 1945 an anti-personnel bomb exploded as it was being clustered. Nine men and eleven women were killed and eleven wounded.

Part of the loading bay, October 1945. The explosion left a shattered building with 40,000 bombs beneath the wreckage. It took three months to clear these highly sensitive bombs and everything to be made safe. Superintendent Gale received the O.B.E., other staff received B.E.M.s and eleven received commendations.

Chemical Laboratories, October 1945. The factory filled 14 million shot for six pounder guns and 20 million anti-tank mines. Ten per cent of all ammunition produced in Britain during the War was made at Kirkby.

Tailors' shop, October 1945. Even without accidental explosions, prolonged exposure to trinitrotoluene (T.N.T.) could be dangerous. The Medical Research Council monitored the health of 62 undergraduates from Oxford University who volunteered to work in the factory for this purpose.

Part of the chemical laboratory, October 1945. One woman who worked in the factory remembered that some chemicals could even bleach hair. The workers received £3 for day shift and £5 for nights.

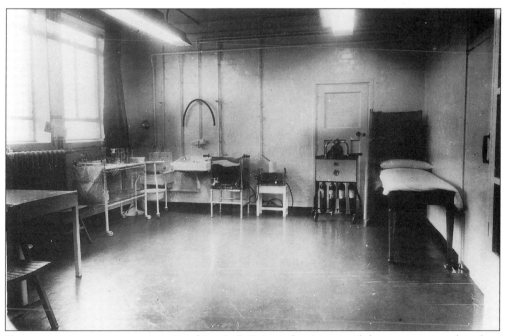

Treatment room, main surgery, October 1945. Four to five Liverpool doctors were employed on a temporary basis until the posts could be filled. Thereafter the factory had five full-time doctors and even a small X-ray unit.

The switchboard, main telephone exchange, October 1945. When the factory closed on 31 March 1946, the keys were handed over to Liverpool Corporation and it became the Kirkby Industrial Estate. One firm employing 600 building workers was already engaged in peace-time work in August 1945.

Boiler House No.1, October 1945. Mr A. Marshall was appointed as Liaison Officer to Liverpool Corporation Industrial Estates and made great efforts to convince firms to settle at Kirkby. Now much extended as part of Knowsley Industrial Estate, it is one of the largest in Britain.

Eight

Nova

Low-rise flats, Tower Hill Estate, Kirkby, 20 February 1970. The beautiful clean lines of this picture show why the design proved so seductive to planners and councillors alike. However, the flats were too small and built of shoddy materials. Universally despised, they are now mostly demolished.

Southdene under construction, from Redhill Avenue, 1952. By the end of the War, bomb damage and slum clearance had made Liverpool's housing shortage acute. In 1947 the Corporation bought Kirkby from the Earl of Sefton for £375,000. Originally the development was to be away from the present town centre and to be continuous with Fazakerley.

Part of Kirkby under construction, 1952. The development was moved to its present position at the insistence of Lancashire County Council — which had been opposed to any Corporation housing in Kirkby, feeling that the whole area should be a designated Green Belt area. They lost this argument, but were able to block some of Liverpool's plans by arguing that the new town should have a chance to develop its own identity, rather than be a mere extension of the city.

Part of Southdene under construction, 1952. Liverpool had to change its plans, and accordingly the three original estates of Kirkby, Northwood, Westvale and Southdene were begun. The elegant plans of Sir Lancelot Keay (including the delightful 'Bath Square') were dropped, and the emphasis was upon speed.

Part of Southdene under construction, 1952. In November 1949 planning permission was granted for the whole of Southdene. The first contract of 674 houses was signed on the 13 March 1952 and thereafter Kirkby became one vast, muddy building site, which it remained for years. In the beginning, houses were constructed at the rate of three a week.

Digmoor Walk, 1952. Twenty months after the first contract was signed, the 1,000th house was handed over to the Corporation. By 1959, 5,000 houses had been completed, by 1961, 10,000.

Rockford Walk, 1952. Such haste caused enormous problems, which were to haunt the new town for decades. Despite the geometric rise in the population, in 1961 there were only eighty shops, and the shortfall was taken up by vans for basic foodstuffs, which, in a world of no competition, meant high prices.

Cherryfield County Junior School, 1954. While the population of the new town was supposedly meant to be the same as its parent city, in fact it was completely unbalanced. While, contrary to popular belief, Kirkby was not used to empty the slums, it was used to accommodate those families who had priority on the housing list. These were exclusively young couples, unskilled or semi-skilled labourers, who traditionally produced large families.

Cherryfield County Junior School, 1955. Before building really took off, the population of Kirkby was 3,078, itself three time what it had been before the War. In 1961 it was 53,139, all young, with projected statistics forecasting it would reach 900,000 by 1991. This placed great strain on the County Education Authority to build schools. Cherryfield was the first to be built since 1806. Five were built in 1956 alone and by 1972 there were thirty two.

Opposite: Coronation celebrations, Quarry Green, 1953. In the centre of the picture is the Vicar, Revd Griffiths, next but one to him on the left is Dr Katie Ainsworth.

Cherryfield County Junior, 1955. Throughout the 1950s and 60s, very few of the population were over thirty years old (in 1961 48 per cent were under fifteen), and they were all working class. Such a social imbalance guaranteed high unemployment, even at times of growth.

Voting at the first Kirkby U.D.C. election, 1958. Until this time Kirkby had the misfortune to be governed by at least six different authorities. The only locally based government was the Parish Council, adequate for the 1,400 inhabitants of the last century, ludicrous for 50,000 people. Accordingly, it became an Urban District Council.

William Byron, Clerk, Kirkby U.D.C. Mr Byron was Clerk for the duration of the Council's existence, from 1958 to 1974.

Kirkby Market, September 1961, opened on the sixth of that month. This was an early triumph for the new council, and did much to remedy the hopelessly inadequate provision of shops.

Shrogs Cottages, Tithebarn Lane, 1959. The building of the new Kirkby naturally meant a loss of the old. The agricultural interest within Lancashire County Council had expressed dismay at the loss of so much excellent land in the late 1940s. The locals, now effectively strangers in their own home town, regretted the loss of the familiar. This site is now an old people's home.

Miss K. Gribble, Children's Librarian, 1968.

Opposite: Kirkby County Library, c. 1964, showing the interior as it originally looked. This was opened in March of that year, bringing much needed recreational and study facilities. At the time, it was the largest public library the County Council possessed.

Miss E.M.E. Brown, Divisional Librarian, with the winners of the poster and essay competition, National Library Week 1966.

The Pigeon House, Ingoe Lane, in a new and previously unimagined world, c. 1960.

County Road, looking north, c. 1960. Alex Chorley's 'great road' of 1696 comes of age.

Harold Wilson, local M.P. and Prime Minister, opens Kirkby Sports Centre, 20 June 1964. Lord Wilson was the Member for the Huyton Constituency from 1948 to 1983, covering the period before Kirkby was developed to after it had become part of Knowsley M.B.C.

Mr and Mrs Wilson at the opening of Kirkby Sports Centre, 20 June 1964. From having virtually no sports facilities, Kirkby went to possessing a stadium capable of accommodating 10,000 spectators.

Kirkby Sports Centre in the process of construction, 1964. It cost £150,000 to build.

Harold Wilson opens Quarry Green Club, 20 July 1968.

Schools' Public Speaking Competition trophy, 1968, presented by Cllr. David Tempest (left).

Webster Park Play Scheme, late 1960s. Webster Park was the first development taken over by the new Urban District Council, 22 February 1960.

Mill Dam, late 1950s, made redundant by new technology and the loss of farms, Kirkby Mill ceased to serve any purpose, and the lake became as it is here. Note the tip in the distance.

Mill Dam, 1977. Mindful of what it had once been like, the Council restored it in 1968.

Cherryfield Heights under construction, 22 September 1959. The first high-rise flats were more of a success than we might suspect with our present jaundiced and disillusioned view. Where properly maintained they remained viable.

The Civic Building under construction, 1967-68. From the ruin of the old Kirkby Hall site arises the new symbol of Kirkby's maturity.

The Civic Building at its opening, 1969.

The Rt. Hon. Harold Wilson, M.P. and Cllr. David Tempest at the opening of Kirkby Civic Building, 1969.

Building of two high rise blocks of flats, 27 September 1960. 'The physical appearance of Kirkby changes every year' said the Clerk, Mr Byron. Built as an overspill estate, Kirkby itself was becoming overcrowded by 1961, so a fourth district was planned, Tower Hill.

Opposite: Tower Hill Estate Shopping Centre, early 1970s. With the building of this estate, modern Kirkby may be regarded as complete. Further development will probably be limited to the rehabilitation of existing dwellings or private housing.

Tower Hill Estate, 4 October 1966. The Minister of Housing, Anthony Greenwood hands over the last house of a 310 house contract to Kirkby U.D.C.

Kirkby Historic Society, National Library Week, 1966. From left to right are; Mr T. Moynahan, Mr M. Hutchingson, Mr Wilson, Mr W.L. French, Mr T. Hills, Mr A. Grant.

Acknowledgements

These photographs are a selection from the extensive collection held by Knowsley M.B.C. at the archives at Kirkby Library. They have been donated over the years by organisations and individuals. The author would especially like to thank the Rt. Hon. The Earl of Derby, Mr Arthur S. Roberts and Mr R. Sharklady for permission to make use of the collections. It is thirty years since the building of Kirkby Library, and twenty since the Local Studies Library was set up at Huyton. In that time many individuals have given photographs, essays and memoirs which have been used in this book, many of these people are no longer with us, or are untraceable at present, so thanks and apologies are due to: Mr T. Walker, Ms Annie Harrison, E. Brown, Mr E. Yates, The Platine Studies, The Reporter Picture Service, The Car, E.O. Shaw. I should also like to thank all those who have written about Kirkby and Knowsley, especially those of the now defunct Historic Society. Further reading may be sought at the Library in the works of Mr Mark Carr, Mr Smith, Mr Plant, Miss Birch, Joan Roberts and many others, all of which have been consulted in the writing of this book.

Stock List

(Titles are listed according to the pre-1974 county boundaries)

BERKSHIRE

Wantage
Irene Hancock
ISBN 0-7524-0146 7

CARDIGANSHIRE

Aberaeron and Mid Ceredigion
William Howells
ISBN 0-7524-0106-8

CHESHIRE

Ashton-under-Lyne and Mossley
Alice Lock
ISBN 0-7524-0164-5

Around Bebington
Pat O'Brien
ISBN 0-7524-0121-1

Crewe
Brian Edge
ISBN 0-7524-0052-5

Frodsham and Helsby
Frodsham and District Local History Group
ISBN 0-7524-0161-0

Macclesfield Silk
Moira Stevenson and Louanne Collins
ISBN 0-7524-0315 X

Marple
Steve Cliffe
ISBN 0-7524-0316-8

Runcorn
Bert Starkey
ISBN 0-7524-0025-8

Warrington
Janice Hayes
ISBN 0-7524-0040-1

West Kirby to Hoylake
Jim O'Neil
ISBN 0-7524-0024-X

Widnes
Anne Hall and the Widnes Historical Society
ISBN 0-7524-0117-3

CORNWALL

Padstow
Malcolm McCarthy
ISBN 0-7524-0033-9

St Ives Bay
Jonathan Holmes
ISBN 0-7524-0186-6

COUNTY DURHAM

Bishop Auckland
John Land
ISBN 0-7524-0312-5

Around Shildon
Vera Chapman
ISBN 0-7524-0115-7

CUMBERLAND

Carlisle
Dennis Perriam
ISBN 0-7524-0166-1

DERBYSHIRE

Around Alfreton
Alfreton and District Heritage Trust
ISBN 0-7524-0041-X

Barlborough, Clowne, Creswell and Whitwell
Les Yaw
ISBN 0-7524-0031-2

Around Bolsover
Bernard Haigh
ISBN 0-7524-0021-5

Around Derby
Alan Champion and Mark Edworthy
ISBN 0-7524-0020-7

Long Eaton
John Barker
ISBN 0-7524-0110-6

Ripley and Codnor
David Buxton
ISBN 0-7524-0042-8

Shirebrook
Geoff Sadler
ISBN 0-7524-0028-2

Shirebrook: A Second Selection
Geoff Sadler
ISBN 0-7524-0317-6

DEVON

Brixham
Ted Gosling and Lyn Marshall
ISBN 0-7524-0037-1

Around Honiton
Les Berry and Gerald Gosling
ISBN 0-7524-0175-0

Around Newton Abbot
Les Berry and Gerald Gosling
ISBN 0-7524-0027-4

Around Ottery St Mary
Gerald Gosling and Peter Harris
ISBN 0-7524-0030-4

Around Sidmouth
Les Berry and Gerald Gosling
ISBN 0-7524-0137-8

DORSET

Around Uplyme and Lyme Regis
Les Berry and Gerald Gosling
ISBN 0-7524-0044-4

ESSEX

Braintree and Bocking
John and Sandra Adlam and Mark Charlton
ISBN 0-7524-0129-7

Ilford
Ian Dowling and Nick Harris
ISBN 0-7524-0050-9

Ilford: A Second Selection
Ian Dowling and Nick Harris
ISBN 0-7524-0320-6

Saffron Walden
Jean Gumbrell
ISBN 0-7524-0176-9

GLAMORGAN

Around Bridgend
Simon Eckley
ISBN 0-7524-0189-0

Caerphilly
Simon Eckley
ISBN 0-7524-0194-7

Around Kenfig Hill and Pyle
Keith Morgan
ISBN 0-7524-0314-1

The County Borough of Merthyr Tydfil
Carolyn Jacob, Stephen Done and Simon Eckley
ISBN 0-7524-0012-6

Mountain Ash, Penrhiwceiber and Abercynon
Bernard Baldwin and Harry Rogers
ISBN 0-7524-0114-9

Pontypridd
Simon Eckley
ISBN 0-7524-0017-7

Rhondda
Simon Eckley and Emrys Jenkins
ISBN 0-7524-0028-2

Rhondda: A Second Selection
Simon Eckley and Emrys Jenkins
ISBN 0-7524-0308-7

Roath, Splott, and Adamsdown
Roath Local History Society
ISBN 0-7524-0199-8

GLOUCESTERSHIRE

Barnwood, Hucclecote and Brockworth
Alan Sutton
ISBN 0-7524-0000-2

Forest to Severn
Humphrey Phelps
ISBN 0-7524-0008-8

Filton and the Flying Machine
Malcolm Hall
ISBN 0-7524-0171-8

Gloster Aircraft Company
Derek James
ISBN 0-7524-0038-X

The City of Gloucester
Jill Voyce
ISBN 0-7524-0306-0

Around Nailsworth and Minchinhampton from the Conway Collection
Howard Beard
ISBN 0-7524-0048-7

Around Newent
Tim Ward
ISBN 0-7524-0003-7

Stroud: Five Stroud Photographers
Howard Beard, Peter Harris and Wilf Merrett
ISBN 0-7524-0305-2

HAMPSHIRE

Gosport
Ian Edelman
ISBN 0-7524-0300-1

Winchester from the Sollars Collection
John Brimfield
ISBN 0-7524-0173-4

HEREFORDSHIRE
Ross-on-Wye
Tom Rigby and Alan Sutton
ISBN 0-7524-0002-9

HERTFORDSHIRE
Buntingford
Philip Plumb
ISBN 0-7524-0170-X

Hampstead Garden Suburb
Mervyn Miller
ISBN 0-7524-0319-2

Hemel Hempstead
Eve Davis
ISBN 0-7524-0167-X

Letchworth
Mervyn Miller
ISBN 0-7524-0318-4

Welwyn Garden City
Angela Eserin
ISBN 0-7524-0133-5

KENT
Hythe
Joy Melville and Angela Lewis-Johnson
ISBN 0-7524-0169-6

North Thanet Coast
Alan Kay
ISBN 0-7524-0112-2

Shorts Aircraft
Mike Hooks
ISBN 0-7524-0193-9

LANCASHIRE
Lancaster and the Lune Valley
Robert Alston
ISBN 0-7524-0015-0

Morecambe Bay
Robert Alston
ISBN 0-7524-0163-7

Manchester
Peter Stewart
ISBN 0-7524-0103-3

LINCOLNSHIRE
Louth
David Cuppleditch
ISBN 0-7524-0172-6

Stamford
David Gerard
ISBN 0-7524-0309-5

LONDON
(Greater London and Middlesex)

Battersea and Clapham
Patrick Loobey
ISBN 0-7524-0010-X

Canning Town
Howard Bloch and Nick Harris
ISBN 0-7524-0057-6

Chiswick
Carolyn and Peter Hammond
ISBN 0-7524-0001-0

Forest Gate
Nick Harris and Dorcas Sanders
ISBN 0-7524-0049-5

Greenwich
Barbara Ludlow
ISBN 0-7524-0045-2

Highgate and Muswell Hill
Joan Schwitzer and Ken Gay
ISBN 0-7524-0119-X

Islington
Gavin Smith
ISBN 0-7524-0140-8

Lewisham
John Coulter and Barry Olley
ISBN 0-7524-0059-2

Leyton and Leytonstone
Keith Romig and Peter Lawrence
ISBN 0-7524-0158-0

Newham Dockland
Howard Bloch
ISBN 0-7524-0107-6

Norwood
Nicholas Reed
ISBN 0-7524-0147-5

Peckham and Nunhead
John D. Beasley
ISBN 0-7524-0122-X

Piccadilly Circus
David Oxford
ISBN 0-7524-0196-3

Stoke Newington
Gavin Smith
ISBN 0-7524-0159-9

Sydenham and Forest Hill
John Coulter and John Seaman
ISBN 0-7524-0036-3

Wandsworth
Patrick Loobey
ISBN 0-7524-0026-6

Wanstead and Woodford
Ian Dowling and Nick Harris
ISBN 0-7524-0113-0

MONMOUTHSHIRE

Vanished Abergavenny
Frank Olding
ISBN 0-7524-0034-7

Abertillery, Aberbeeg and Llanhilleth
Abertillery and District Museum Society and Simon Eckley
ISBN 0-7524-0134-3

Blaina, Nantyglo and Brynmawr
Trevor Rowson
ISBN 0-7524-0136-X

NORFOLK

North Norfolk
Cliff Richard Temple
ISBN 0-7524-0149-1

NOTTINGHAMSHIRE

Nottingham 1897–1947
Douglas Whitworth
ISBN 0-7524-0157-2

OXFORDSHIRE

Banbury
Tom Rigby
ISBN 0-7524-0013-4

PEMBROKESHIRE

Saundersfoot and Tenby
Ken Daniels
ISBN 0-7524-0192-0

RADNORSHIRE

Llandrindod Wells
Chris Wilson
ISBN 0-7524-0191-2

SHROPSHIRE

Leominster
Eric Turton
ISBN 0-7524-0307-9

Ludlow
David Lloyd
ISBN 0-7524-0155-6

Oswestry
Bernard Mitchell
ISBN 0-7524-0032-0

North Telford: Wellington, Oakengates, and Surrounding Areas
John Powell and Michael A. Vanns
ISBN 0-7524-0124-6

South Telford: Ironbridge Gorge, Madeley, and Dawley
John Powell and Michael A. Vanns
ISBN 0-7524-0125-4

SOMERSET

Bath
Paul De'Ath
ISBN 0-7524-0127-0

Around Yeovil
Robin Ansell and Marion Barnes
ISBN 0-7524-0178-5

STAFFORDSHIRE

Cannock Chase
Sherry Belcher and Mary Mills
ISBN 0-7524-0051-7

Around Cheadle
George Short
ISBN 0-7524-0022-3

The Potteries
Ian Lawley
ISBN 0-7524-0046-0

East Staffordshire
Geoffrey Sowerby and Richard Farman
ISBN 0-7524-0197-1

SUFFOLK

Lowestoft to Southwold
Humphrey Phelps
ISBN 0-7524-0108-4

Walberswick to Felixstowe
Humphrey Phelps
ISBN 0-7524-0109-2

SURREY

Around Camberley
Ken Clarke
ISBN 0-7524-0148-3

Around Cranleigh
Michael Miller
ISBN 0-7524-0143-2

Epsom and Ewell
Richard Essen
ISBN 0-7524-0111-4

Farnham by the Wey
Jean Parratt
ISBN 0-7524-0185-8

Industrious Surrey: Historic Images of the County at Work
Chris Shepheard
ISBN 0-7524-0009-6

Reigate and Redhill
Mary G. Goss
ISBN 0-7524-0179-3

Richmond and Kew
Richard Essen
ISBN 0-7524-0145-9

SUSSEX

Billingshurst
Wendy Lines
ISBN 0-7524-0301-X

WARWICKSHIRE

Central Birmingham 1870–1920
Keith Turner
ISBN 0-7524-0053-3

Old Harborne
Roy Clarke
ISBN 0-7524-0054-1

WILTSHIRE

Malmesbury
Dorothy Barnes
ISBN 0-7524-0177-7

Great Western Swindon
Tim Bryan
ISBN 0-7524-0153-X

Midland and South Western Junction Railway
Mike Barnsley and Brian Bridgeman
ISBN 0-7524-0016-9

WORCESTERSHIRE

Around Malvern
Keith Smith
ISBN 0-7524-0029-0

YORKSHIRE
(EAST RIDING)

Hornsea
G.L. Southwell
ISBN 0-7524-0120-3

YORKSHIRE
(NORTH RIDING)

Northallerton
Vera Chapman
ISBN 0-7524-055-X

Scarborough in the 1970s and 1980s
Richard Percy
ISBN 0-7524-0325-7

YORKSHIRE
(WEST RIDING)

Barnsley
Barnsley Archive Service
ISBN 0-7524-0188-2

Bingley
Bingley and District Local History Society
ISBN 0-7524-0311-7

Bradford
Gary Firth
ISBN 0-7524-0313-3

Castleford
Wakefield Metropolitan District Council
ISBN 0-7524-0047-9

Doncaster
Peter Tuffrey
ISBN 0-7524-0162-9

Harrogate
Malcolm Neesam
ISBN 0-7524-0154-8

Holme Valley
Peter and Iris Bullock
ISBN 0-7524-0139-4

Horsforth
Alan Cockroft and Matthew Young
ISBN 0-7524-0130-0

Knaresborough
Arnold Kellett
ISBN 0-7524-0131-9

Around Leeds
Matthew Young and Dorothy Payne
ISBN 0-7524-0168-8

Penistone
Matthew Young and David Hambleton
ISBN 0-7524-0138-6

Selby from the William Rawling Collection
Matthew Young
ISBN 0-7524-0198-X

Central Sheffield
Martin Olive
ISBN 0-7524-0011-8

Around Stocksbridge
Stocksbridge and District History Society
ISBN 0-7524-0165-3

TRANSPORT

Filton and the Flying Machine
Malcolm Hall
ISBN 0-7524-0171-8

Gloster Aircraft Company
Derek James
ISBN 0-7524-0038-X

Great Western Swindon
Tim Bryan
ISBN 0-7524-0153-X

Midland and South Western Junction Railway
Mike Barnsley and Brian Bridgeman
ISBN 0-7524-0016-9

Shorts Aircraft
Mike Hooks
ISBN 0-7524-0193-9

This stock list shows all titles available in the United Kingdom as at 30 September 1995.

ORDER FORM

The books in this stock list are available from your local bookshop. Alternatively they are available by mail order at a totally inclusive price of £10.00 per copy.

For overseas orders please add the following postage supplement for each copy ordered:
      European Union £0.36 (this includes the Republic of Ireland)
      Royal Mail Zone 1 (for example, U.S.A. and Canada) £1.96
      Royal Mail Zone 2 (for example, Australia and New Zealand) £2.47

Please note that all of these supplements are actual Royal Mail charges with no profit element to the Chalford Publishing Company. Furthermore, as the Air Mail Printed Papers rate applies, we are restricted from enclosing any personal correspondence other than to indicate the senders name.

Payment can be made by cheque, Visa or Mastercard. Please indicate your method of payment on this order form.

If you are not entirely happy with your purchase you may return it within 30 days of receipt for a full refund.

Please send your order to:

      The Chalford Publishing Company,
      St Mary's Mill,
      Chalford,
      Stroud,
      Gloucestershire
      GL6 8NX

This order form should perforate away from the book. However, if you are reluctant to damage the book in any way we are quite happy to accept a photocopy order form or a letter containing the necessary information.

PLEASE WRITE CLEARLY USING BLOCK CAPITALS

Name and address of the person ordering the books listed below:

_____

_____

_____ Post code _____

Please also supply your telephone number in case we have difficulty fully understanding your requirements.   Tel.: _____ - _____

Name and address of where the books are to be despatched to (if different from above):

_____

_____

_____ Post code _____

Please indicate here if you would like to receive future information on books published by the Chalford Publishing Company.
____ Yes, please put me on your mailing list   ____ No, please just send the books ordered below

Title	ISBN	Quantity
....	0-7524-_____-___	_____
....	0-7524-_____-___	_____
....	0-7524-_____-___	_____
....	0-7524-_____-___	_____
....	0-7524-_____-___	_____
	Total number of books	_____

Cost of books delivered in UK = Number of books ordered @ £10 each =£ _____

Overseas postage supplement (if relevant)   =£ _____

TOTAL PAYMENT   =£ _____

Method of Payment   ❏ Cheque   ❏ Visa   ❏ Mastercard   **VISA**

Please make cheques payable to *The Chalford Publishing Company*   MasterCard

Name of Card Holder   _____

Card Number ❏❏❏❏❏❏❏❏❏❏❏❏❏❏❏❏❏❏❏❏

Expiry date ❏❏ / ❏❏

I authorise payment of £_____ from the above card

Signed _____